The Irish Get U

ISBN

Published in Ireland by
GET UP AND GO PUBLICATIONS LTD
Camboline, Hazelwood, Sligo, F91 NP04, Ireland.
Email: info@getupandgodiary.com
www.getupandgodiary.com

Compiled by Eileen Forrestal
Graphic design by Nuala Redmond
Illustrations: dreamstime.com; shutterstock.com
Printed in Ireland by GPS Colour Graphics.

*May you have warm words
on a cold evening,
a full moon on a dark night,
and the road downhill
all the way to your door.*

Copyright c 2007-2020 Get Up And Go Publications Ltd.

All rights reserved. No part of this publication may be reproduced, stored in, or introduced into, a retrieval system, or transmitted in any form, or by any means (electronic, mechanical, scanning, recording or otherwise) without the prior permission of the Publisher. Any person who does any unauthorised act in relation to this publication may be liable to criminal prosecution and civil claim for damages.

2020 BANK AND PUBLIC HOLIDAYS

REPUBLIC OF IRELAND
New Year's Day, 1 January;
St Patrick's Day, 17 March;
Good Friday, 10 April;
Easter Monday, 13 April;
May Day Bank Holiday, 4 May;
June Bank Holiday, 1 June;
August Bank Holiday, 3 August;
October Bank Holiday, 26 October;
Christmas Day, 25 December;
St Stephen's Day, 26 December.

NORTHERN IRELAND
New Year's Day, 1 January;
Good Friday, 10 April;
May Day Holiday, 4 May;
Orangemen's Holiday, 13 July;
Christmas Day, 25 December;

St Patrick's Day, 17 March;
Easter Monday, 13 April;
Spring Bank Holiday, 25 May;
Summer Bank Holiday, 31 August;
Boxing Day, 26 December.

ENGLAND, SCOTLAND AND WALES
New Year's Day, 1 January;
Easter Monday, 13 April;
May Day Holiday, 4 May;
Summer Bank Holiday, 31 August;
Christmas Day, 25 December;

Good Friday, 10 April;
St George's Day, 23 April
Spring Bank Holiday, 25 May;
Remembrance Sunday, 8 November;
Boxing Day, 26 December.

UNITED STATES OF AMERICA
New Year's Day, 1 January;
Presidents' Day, 17 February;
Independence Day, 4 July;
Columbus Day, 12 October;
Thanksgiving Day, 26 November;

Martin Luther King Day, 20 January;
Memorial Day, 25 May;
Labour Day, 7 September;
Veterans Day, 11 November;
Christmas Day, 25 December.

CANADA
New Year's Day, 1 January;
Heritage Day, 17 February;
St Patrick's Day, 17 March;
Easter Monday, 13 April;
Canada Day, 1 July;
Thanksgiving Day, 12 October;
Christmas Day, 25 December;

Family Day, 17 February;
Commonwealth Day, 9 March;
Good Friday, 10 April;
Victoria Day 18 May;
Labour Day, 7 September;
Rememberance Day, 11 November;
Boxing Day, 26 December.

AUSTRALIA (NATIONAL HOLIDAYS)
New Year's Day, 1 January;
Good Friday, 10 April;
Anzac Day 25 April;
Christmas Day, 25 December;

Australia Day, 27 January;
Easter Monday, 13 April;
Queen's Birthday, 8 June;
Boxing Day, 26 December.

2020 CALENDAR

January
S	M	T	W	T	F	S
			1	2	3	4
5	6	7	8	9	10	11
12	13	14	15	16	17	18
19	20	21	22	23	24	25
26	27	28	29	30	31	

February
S	M	T	W	T	F	S
						1
2	3	4	5	6	7	8
9	10	11	12	13	14	15
16	17	18	19	20	21	22
23	24	25	26	27	28	29

March
S	M	T	W	T	F	S
1	2	3	4	5	6	7
8	9	10	11	12	13	14
15	16	17	18	19	20	21
22	23	24	25	26	27	28
29	30	31				

April
S	M	T	W	T	F	S
			1	2	3	4
5	6	7	8	9	10	11
12	13	14	15	16	17	18
19	20	21	22	23	24	25
26	27	28	29	30		

May
S	M	T	W	T	F	S
					1	2
3	4	5	6	7	8	9
10	11	12	13	14	15	16
17	18	19	20	21	22	23
24	25	26	27	28	29	30
31						

June
S	M	T	W	T	F	S
	1	2	3	4	5	6
7	8	9	10	11	12	13
14	15	16	17	18	19	20
21	22	23	24	25	26	27
28	29	30				

July
S	M	T	W	T	F	S
			1	2	3	4
5	6	7	8	9	10	11
12	13	14	15	16	17	18
19	20	21	22	23	24	25
26	27	28	29	30	31	

August
S	M	T	W	T	F	S
						1
2	3	4	5	6	7	8
9	10	11	12	13	14	15
16	17	18	19	20	21	22
23	24	25	26	27	28	29
30	31					

September
S	M	T	W	T	F	S
		1	2	3	4	5
6	7	8	9	10	11	12
13	14	15	16	17	18	19
20	21	22	23	24	25	26
27	28	29	30			

October
S	M	T	W	T	F	S
				1	2	3
4	5	6	7	8	9	10
11	12	13	14	15	16	17
18	19	20	21	22	23	24
25	26	27	28	29	30	31

November
S	M	T	W	T	F	S
1	2	3	4	5	6	7
8	9	10	11	12	13	14
15	16	17	18	19	20	21
22	23	24	25	26	27	28
29	30					

December
S	M	T	W	T	F	S
		1	2	3	4	5
6	7	8	9	10	11	12
13	14	15	16	17	18	19
20	21	22	23	24	25	26
27	28	29	30	31		

Forgive the past – let it go
Live the present – the power of now
Create the future – thoughts become things

Dear Reader,

We are delighted that you're holding this Get Up and Go diary in your hands today. You are about to embark on a wonderful journey with 'the world's best loved transformational diary'.

Whether this is your first Get Up and Go diary or you're a regular and loyal customer, we thank you, and we trust that you will benefit from the carefully chosen words contained herein.

You may have chosen this diary for yourself or received it as gift from a friend; either way, we know it will fill your days with inspiration, encouragement, motivation and empowerment in the year ahead.

You may also like to follow us on Facebook, Twitter and Instagram for additional timely words of inspiration and encouragement. Please check out our website **www.getupandgodiary.com** where you can find out about (and purchase) new products, follow our blog, learn about upcoming events and see details of special offers.

Also there's something extra we think you'll appreciate. Through our partnership with the Global Giving Initiative www.B1G1.com this diary is changing lives – a contribution from each Get Up and Go diary goes towards providing children in rural Cambodia with access to clean water, children in rural India enjoying e-learning and we're helping to build a school in Kenya. You'll see more about all of that on our webite.

And it all happens because people like you love their Get Up and Go diary. Thank you so much for being one of them.

With very best wishes for the year ahead,

Brendan Sands

Eileen Forrestal

This diary belongs to: _____

Address: _____

Tel: _____   Email: _____

Emergency telephone number: _____

spriocanna
GOALS

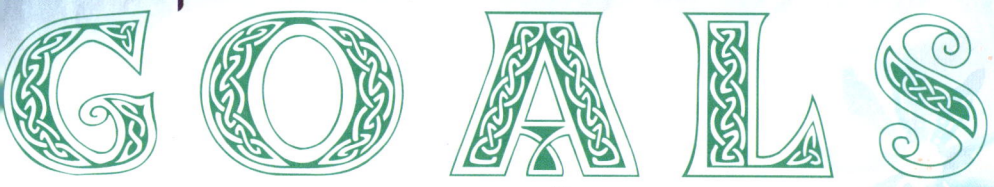

EANÁIR
JANUARY

_____
_____
_____
_____
_____
_____
_____
_____
_____
_____
_____

*Nuair a bhíonn an fíon istigh,
bíonn an ciall amuigh.*
When the wine is in, the sense is out.

**Is fearr Gaeilge briste,
ná Béarla cliste.**
Broken Irish is better than
clever English.

> Hope smiles from the threshold of the year to come, whispering, 'It will be happier.'
>
> *Alfred Lord Tennyson*

JANUARY

Happy New Year

> Your thoughts are like the seeds you plant in your garden. Your beliefs are like the soil in which you plant the seeds.
>
> *Louise Hay*

WEDNESDAY 1
HAPPY NEW YEAR!

Start as you mean to go on

> *The object of a new year is not that we should have a new year. It is that we should have a new soul.*
>
> GK Chesterton

Perhaps the art of harvesting the secret riches of our lives is best achieved when we place profound trust in the act of beginning. Risk might be our greatest ally. To live a truly creative life, we always need to cast a critical look at where we presently are, attempting always to discern where we have become stagnant and where new beginning might be ripening. There can be no growth if we do not remain open and vulnerable to what is new and different. I have never seen anyone take a risk for growth that was not rewarded a thousand times over.

John O'Donohue

THURSDAY 2

There are (at least) two sides to every story

FRIDAY 3

Be willing to wonder

JANUARY

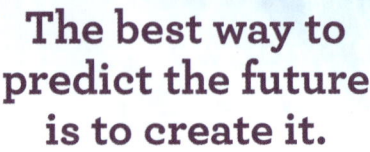

The best way to predict the future is to create it.
R Drucker

If you want a new tomorrow, then make new choices today.
Tim Fargo

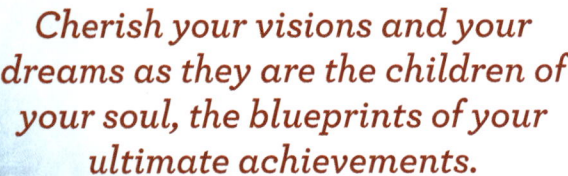

Cherish your visions and your dreams as they are the children of your soul, the blueprints of your ultimate achievements.
Napoleon Hill

SATURDAY 4

Write a letter to someone you miss

SUNDAY 5

What you do now matters

OUR DEEPEST FEAR

Our deepest fear is not that we are inadequate.
Our deepest fear is that we are powerful beyond measure.
It is our light, not our darkness
That most frightens us. We ask ourselves
Who am I to be brilliant, gorgeous, talented, fabulous?
Actually, who are you not to be?
You are a child of God. Your playing small
Does not serve the world.
There's nothing enlightened about shrinking
So that other people won't feel insecure around you.
We are all meant to shine,
As children do.
We were born to make manifest
The glory of God that is within us.
It's not just in some of us; It's in everyone.
And as we let our own light shine,
We unconsciously give other people
permission to do the same.
As we're liberated from our own fear,
Our presence automatically liberates others.

Marianne Williamson

*Go confidently in the direction of your dreams.
Live the life you have imagined.*

Henry David Thoreau

JANUARY

MONDAY 6

See beauty in unexpected places

TUESDAY 7

Let your desires, not your fears, be your guide

Accept that some days you're the pigeon and some days you're the statue.

Do not seek to follow in the footsteps of the wise; instead, seek what they sought.
Matuso Basho

It is not true that people stop pursuing dreams because they grow old, they grow old because they stop pursuing dreams.
Gabriel García Márquez

The reasonable man adapts himself to the world; the unreasonable one persists in trying to adapt the world to himself. Therefore all progress depends on the unreasonable man.
George Bernard Shaw

WEDNESDAY 8

Sort out your priorities

THURSDAY 9

Remember what's important

FRIDAY 10

It pays to listen

SATURDAY 11

Add value wherever you are

SUNDAY 12

Lighten up; it may not happen!

JANUARY

MONDAY 13

Consider the consequences

TUESDAY 14

Acknowledge others for the contribution they make

It is during our darkest moments that we must focus to see the light.

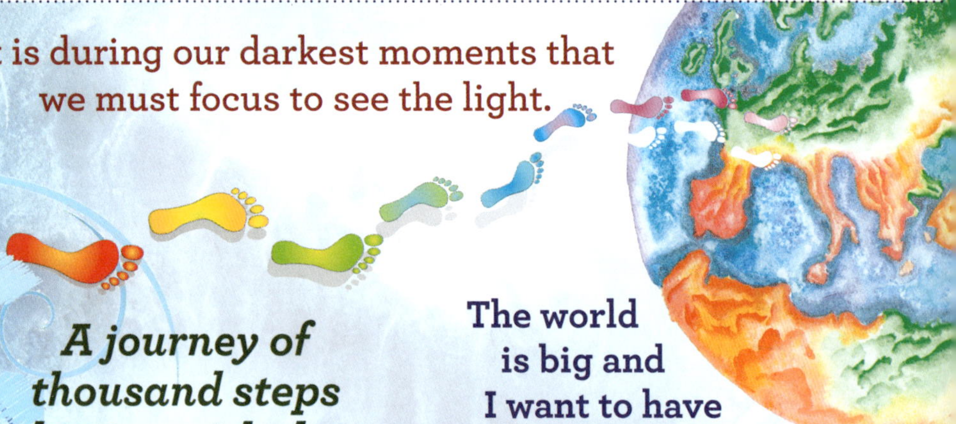

A journey of thousand steps begins with the first step.
Chinese proverb

The world is big and I want to have a good look at it before it gets dark.
John Muir

WEDNESDAY 15

Stop trying to please everyone

Every new beginning comes from some other beginning's end.
Seneca

Do you want to know who you are? Don't ask. Act! Action will delineate and define you.
Thomas Jefferson

THURSDAY 16

Prepare thoughtfully

FRIDAY 17

Be grateful for lessons learned

SATURDAY 18

Here is the only place on earth to be

SUNDAY 19

Ask people what they want, really

JANUARY

THE MAN WHO THINKS HE CAN

If you think you are beaten, you are;
If you think that you dare not, you don't.
If you'd like to win, but you think you can't,
It's almost certain you won't.
If you think you'll lose, you've lost;
For out in the world you'll find
Success begins with a fellow's will –
It's all in the state of mind.
If you think you're out-classed, you are;
You've got to think high to rise.
You've got to be sure of yourself before
You can ever win a prize.
Life's battles don't always go
To the stronger or faster man;
But sooner or later, the man who wins
Is the man who thinks he can!

Walter D Wintle

MONDAY **20**

A friends eye is a good mirror

TUESDAY **21**

Be realistic – plan for a miracle!

May there be kindness in your gaze when you look within.
John O'Donohue

WEDNESDAY 22

Turn your melodrama into a mellow drama

THURSDAY 23

Don't waste energy arguing with reality

FRIDAY 24

Be willing to try and fail and try again

SATURDAY 25

Ask new questions

SUNDAY 26

Look within, not without

MONDAY 27

Concentrate on the outcome you desire

TUESDAY 28

Place high value on the truth

WEDNESDAY 29

Do something special for a loved one today

THURSDAY 30

Declutter your space — inside and out

FRIDAY 31

Maintain a childlike heart

Between what is said and not meant, and what is meant and not said, most of love is lost.
K Gibran

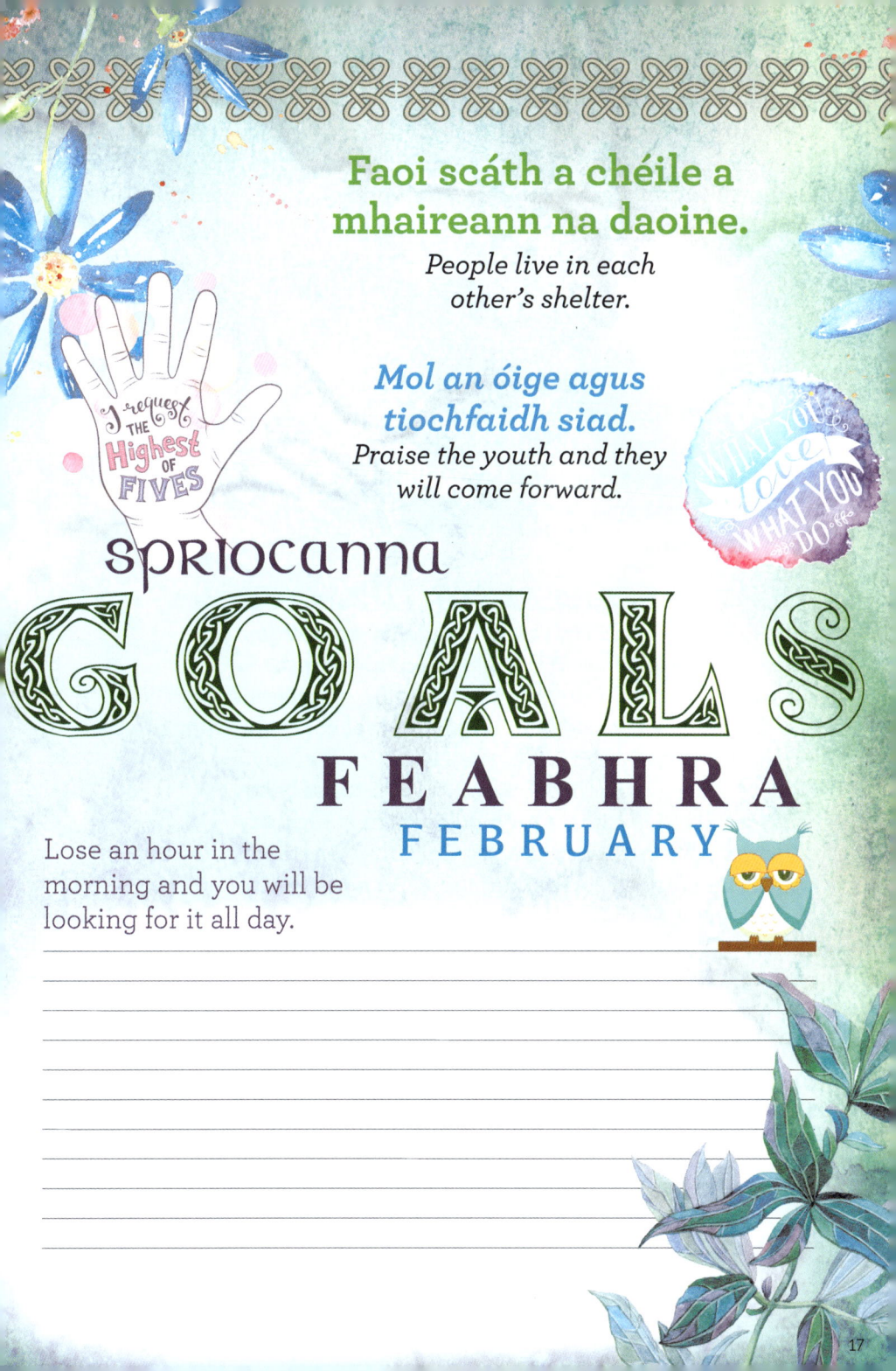

Faoi scáth a chéile a mhaireann na daoine.
People live in each other's shelter.

Mol an óige agus tiochfaidh siad.
Praise the youth and they will come forward.

spriocanna
GOALS
FEABHRA
FEBRUARY

Lose an hour in the morning and you will be looking for it all day.

ABOUT CHILDREN

Your children are not your children.
They are the sons and daughters of life's longing
for itself. They come through you but not from you.
And though they are with you yet they belong not to you.
You may give them your love but not your thoughts,
for they have their own thoughts. You may house
their bodies, but not their souls, For their souls
dwell in the house of tomorrow, which you
cannot visit, not even in your dreams.
You may strive to be like them, but seek not
to make them like you, for life goes not
backwards nor tarries with yesterday.
You are the bows from which your children,
as living arrows, are sent forth.

Kahlil Gibran

CHILDREN LEARN WHAT THEY LIVE

If children live with criticism, they learn to condemn.
If children live with hostility, they learn to fight.
If children live with fear, they learn to be apprehensive.
If children live with pity, they learn to feel sorry for themselves.
If children live with ridicule, they learn to feel shy.
If children live with jealousy, they learn to feel envy.
If children live with shame, they learn to feel guilty.
If children live with encouragement, they learn confidence.
If children live with tolerance, they learn patience.
If children live with praise, they learn appreciation.
If children live with acceptance, they learn to love.
If children live with approval, they learn to like themselves.
If children live with recognition, they learn it is good to have a goal.
If children live with sharing, they learn generosity.
If children live with honesty, they learn truthfulness.
If children live with fairness, they learn justice.
If children live with kindness and consideration,
they learn respect.
If children live with security, they learn to have
faith in themselves and in those about them.
If children live with friendliness, they learn
the world is a nice place in which to live.

Dorothy Law Nolte

FEBRUARY

When one door closes, another opens; but we often look so long and so regretfully upon the closed door that we do not see the one that has opened for us.

Alexander Graham Bell

Those who are easily shocked, should be shocked more often.

Mae West

I try to make my mood uplifting and peaceful, then watch the world around me reflect that mood.

Yaya DaCosta

SATURDAY 1

Make a wish list and put it where you can see it

SUNDAY 2

There is something to learn in every situation

MY FURRY FRIEND

What would I do without you,
My precious, furry friend?
Part mischief, but all blessing,
And faithful to the end!
You look at me with eyes of love;
You never hold a grudge . . .
You think I'm far too wonderful
To criticise or judge.
It seems your greatest joy in life
Is being close to me . . .
I think God knew how comforting
Your warm, soft fur would be.
I know you think you're human,
But I'm glad it isn't true . . .
The world would be a nicer place
If folks were more like you!
A few short years are all we have;
One day we'll have to part . . .
But you, my pet, will always have
A place within my heart.

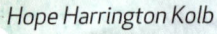

Hope Harrington Kolb

**For every minute you are angry you
lose sixty seconds of happiness.**

Ralph Waldo Emerson

FEBRUARY

*It's not the score that makes us great,
Nor is it the wealth we strive to create,
But that we live our lives
in pursuit of the truth,
And honour the dreams
we dreamt in our youth.*

Mike Dooley

dream on...

MONDAY 3

Have compassion for your inner child

TUESDAY 4

The future is yours to design

WEDNESDAY 5

Reawaken your enthusiasm for living

Love is like a beautiful flower which I may not touch, but whose fragrance makes the garden a place of delight just the same.

Helen Keller

FEBRUARY

THURSDAY 6

Being true to yourself is always the best option

FRIDAY 7

Get up early and witness the sunrise

SATURDAY 8

Avoid negative influences in your life

> A constructive, useful life, good works, and good relationships are as valid as writing poetry or inventing a machine. Anything that one does well and obtains satisfaction from, is a good enough reason for living. To be a decent human being that people like and feel better for knowing, is enough.
> *Robert Gould*

SUNDAY 9

Go and breathe where the air is fresh

> **To have courage for whatever comes in life – everything lies in that.**
> *St Teresa of Avila*

MONDAY 10

Trust divine timing

TUESDAY 11

A poor workman blames his tools

WEDNESDAY 12

Stretch your body and your mind

THURSDAY 13

Do something unexpected – surprise yourself

Love is friendship that has caught fire. It is quiet understanding, mutual confidence, sharing and forgiving. It is loyalty through good and bad times. It settles for less than perfection and makes allowances for human weaknesses.
Ann Landers

FEBRUARY

The highest result of education is tolerance.
Helen Keller

FRIDAY 14
St Valentine's Day

Get to the heart of the matter

Too often we underestimate the power of a touch, a smile, a kind word, a listening ear, an honest compliment, or the smallest act of caring, all of which have the potential to turn a life around.
Leo Buscaglia

SATURDAY 15

Take time to notice what's going on around you

SUNDAY 16

It's ok to say no sometimes

> We should give as we would receive, cheerfully, quickly, and without hesitation; for there is no grace in a benefit that sticks to the fingers.
>
> *Seneca*

MONDAY 17

Dance lightly with life

TUESDAY 18

Do your best and be satisfied

WEDNESDAY 19

The more things change the more they stay the same

THURSDAY 20

Extend your compassion to all of nature

Regret for wasted time is more wasted time.
Mason Cooley

I have found that if you love life, life will love you back.

Arthur Rubinstein

FRIDAY 21

You are lovable, loving and loved

SATURDAY 22

Follow your own star

SUNDAY 23

Trust your inner compass

Climb the mountain not to plant your flag, but to embrace the challenge, enjoy the air and behold the view. Climb it so you can see the world, not so the world can see you.
David McCullough Jr

I didn't ask for it to be over, but then again, I never asked for it to begin. For that is the way it is with life, as some of the most beautiful days come completely by chance. And even the most beautiful days eventually have their sunsets.

FEBRUARY

Until the great mass of the people shall be filled with the sense of responsibility for each other's welfare, social justice can never be attained.

Helen Keller

MONDAY 24

Contentment is a pearl of great value

TUESDAY 25

Overnight success doesn't happen overnight

WEDNESDAY 26

Every cloud has a silver lining

THURSDAY 27

Opportunity can knock very softly

FEBRUARY

FRIDAY 28

Do not dismiss your dreams

SATURDAY 29

Put yourself on the top of your commitment list

Life moves on, whether we act as cowards or heroes. Life has no other discipline to impose, if we would but realise it, than to accept life unquestioningly. Everything we shut our eyes to, everything we run away from, everything we deny, denigrate or despise, serves to defeat us in the end. What seems nasty, painful or evil can become a source of beauty, joy and strength, if faced with an open mind. Every moment is a golden one for those who have the vision to recognise it as such.

Henry Millar

One of the biggest mistakes we make is thinking that other people think the way we think.

spriocanna
GOALS
MÁRTA
MARCH

_____
_____
_____
_____
_____
_____
_____
_____

You've got to do your own growing, no matter how tall your grandfather was.

Níl saoi gan locht.
There's no sage without a fault.

An té nach bhfuil láidir, ní foláir dó bheith glic.
He who is not strong must be clever.

JUST START

SUNDAY **1**

Simplify your life

MARCH

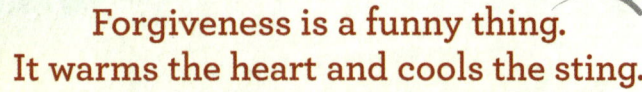

Forgiveness is a funny thing.
It warms the heart and cools the sting.
William Arthur Ward

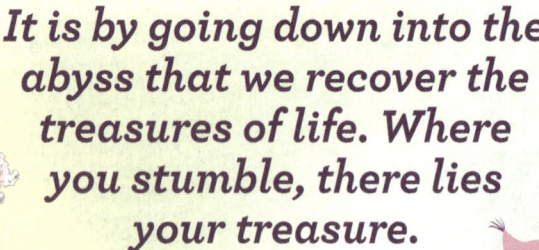

It is by going down into the abyss that we recover the treasures of life. Where you stumble, there lies your treasure.
Joseph Campbell

MONDAY 2

What are you resisting?

All the powers in the universe are already ours. It is we who have put our hands over our eyes and cry that it is dark.
Swami Vivekananda

TUESDAY 3

Connect with friends – new and old

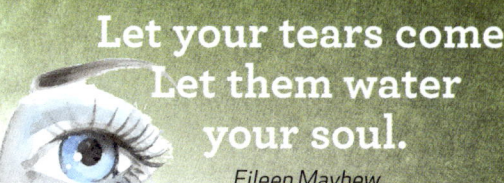

> Let your tears come.
> Let them water
> your soul.
>
> Eileen Mayhew

> Live this day as if it will be your last.
> Remember that you will only find "tomorrow"
> on the calendars of fools. Forget yesterday's
> defeats and ignore the problems of tomorrow.
> This is all you have. Make it the best day of your
> year. The saddest words you can ever utter are
> "If I had my life to live over again..."
> Take the baton, now.
> Run with it!
> This is your day!
> Beginning today,
> treat everyone you meet,
> friend or foe, loved
> one or stranger,
> as if they were going to be dead at midnight.
> Extend to each person, no matter how trivial
> the contact, all the care and kindness and
> understanding and love that you can muster,
> and do it with no thought of any reward.
> Your life will never be the same again.
>
> Og Mandino

> What we have once enjoyed we
> can never lose. All that we love
> deeply, becomes a part of us.
>
> Helen Keller

The bitterest tears shed over
graves are for words left unsaid
and deeds left undone.

Harriet Beecher Stowe

Those we love don't go away,
They walk beside us every day.
Unseen, unheard, but always near.
Still loved, still missed, and ever here.

The person who tries to live alone will not succeed as a human being. His heart withers if it does not answer another heart. His mind shrinks away if he hears only the echoes of his own thoughts and finds no other inspiration.

Pearl S Buck

WEDNESDAY 4

Meditate for a quiet mind

THURSDAY 5

Stand up for what is right

MARCH

> *Once I knew only darkness and stillness ... my life was without past or future... but a little word from the fingers of another fell into my hand that clutched at emptiness, and my heart leaped to the rapture of living.*
>
> *Helen Keller*

FRIDAY 6

However good or bad the situation, it will change

SATURDAY 7

Everyone deserves to be heard

SUNDAY 8

This is how it turned out

MARCH

Today, give yourself permission to be outrageously kind, irrationally warm, improbably generous. I promise it will be a blast.

Sasha Dicter

MONDAY 9

Be open to another point of view

REMEMBERED JOY

*I could not stay another day
To love, to laugh, to work or play.
Tasks left undone must stay that way
And if my parting has left a void,
Then fill it with remembered joy.*

Start by doing what's necessary, then do what's possible, and suddenly you're doing the impossible.

St Francis Of Assisi

TUESDAY 10

Use the power of your imagination positively

> What can a pencil do for all of us? Amazing things. It can write transcendent poetry, uplifting music, or life-changing equations; it can sketch the future, give life to untold beauty, and communicate the full-force of our love and aspirations.
>
> *Adam Braun*

WEDNESDAY 11

Ignore those who try to discourage you

THURSDAY 12

Keep your promises

FRIDAY 13

Open your eyes and see things as they really are

> So when you are listening to somebody, completely, attentively, then you are listening not only to the words, but also to the feeling of what is being conveyed, to the whole of it, not part of it.
>
> *Jiddu Krishnamurti*

MARCH

SATURDAY 14

Be honourable in all your dealings

AS YOU GO THROUGH LIFE

Don't look for the flaws as you go through life;
And even when you find them,
It is wise and kind to be somewhat blind
And look for the virtue behind them.
For the cloudiest night has a hint of light
Somewhere in its shadows hiding;
It is better by far to hunt for a star,
Than the spots on the sun abiding.
The current of life runs ever away
To the bosom of God's great ocean.
Don't set your force 'gainst the river's course
And think to alter its motion.
Don't waste a curse on the universe –
Remember it lived before you.
Don't butt at the storm with your puny form,
But bend and let it go o'er you.
The world will never adjust itself
To suit your whims to the letter.
Some things must go wrong your whole life long,
And the sooner you know it the better.
It is folly to fight with the Infinite,
And go under at last in the wrestle;
The wiser man shapes into God's plan
As water shapes into a vessel.

Ella Wheeler Wilcox

SUNDAY 15

Self-expression is essential to life

> **A man loves his sweetheart the most, his wife the best, but his mother the longest.**
>
> *Irish Proverb*

MONDAY 16

Be a seeker of wisdom and truth

TUESDAY 17
Bank holiday
☘ St Patricks Day

Begin with the next first step

WEDNESDAY 18

Challenge the limits of your own thinking

THURSDAY 19

Life is too important to be taken seriously

FRIDAY 20

Gratitude is a miraculous attitude

MARCH

NOBODY KNOWS BUT MOTHER

Nobody knows of the work it makes
To keep the home together,
Nobody knows of the steps it takes,
Nobody knows – but mother.

Nobody listens to childish woes,
Which kisses only smother;
Nobody's pained by naughty blows,
Nobody – only mother.

Nobody knows of the sleepless care
Bestowed on baby brother;
Nobody knows of the tender prayer,
Nobody – only mother.

Nobody knows of the lessons taught
Of loving one another;
Nobody knows of the patience sought,
Nobody – only mother.

Nobody knows of the anxious fears,
Lest darlings may not weather
The storm of life in after years,
Nobody knows – but mother.

Nobody kneels at the throne above
To thank the Heavenly Father
For that sweetest gift –
a mother's love;
Nobody can –
but mother.

Author unknown

SATURDAY 21

Happy times are best shared

SUNDAY 22
Mother's Day

You don't know what you've got till it's gone

> Take out another notebook, pick up another pen and just write, just write, just write. In the middle of the world, make one positive step. In the centre of chaos, make one definitive act. Just write. Say yes, stay alive, be awake. Just write. Just write. Just write.
>
> *Natalie Goldberg*

MONDAY **23**

Join an exercise class

TUESDAY **24**

Understand yourself and you will understand others

WEDNESDAY **25**

Think big thoughts but acknowledge small actions

THURSDAY **26**

Strive for excellence over perfection

FRIDAY 27

We all have more potential than we could ever know

SATURDAY 28

Focus on making things better

SUNDAY 29

Be willing to let go of childish ways

MONDAY 30

Stay true to your life's purpose

TUESDAY 31

Learn to be powerful in the face of uncertainty

Nothing can bring you peace but yourself.

Ralph Waldo Emerson

spriocanna
GOALS

AIBREÁN
APRIL

Filleann an feall ar an bhfeallaire.
The treachery returns to the betrayer.

Is fearr an tsláinte ná na táinte.
Health is better than wealth.

May peace and plenty bless your world with joy that long endures.

hello SPRING

APRIL

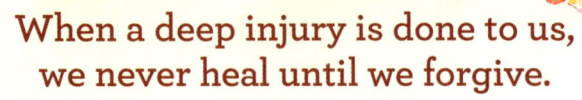

> When a deep injury is done to us, we never heal until we forgive.
> *Nelson Mandela*

> I not only use all the dreams I have, but all that I can borrow.
> *Woodrow Wilson*

> *The privilege of a lifetime is being who you are.*
> *Joseph Campbell*

WEDNESDAY 1

Fear begins in the mind

THURSDAY 2

What are you putting of?

FRIDAY 3

Learn to breathe

SATURDAY 4

Patience is a virtue

I hope you live louder.
I hope you laugh more.
I hope you sing at the top of your lungs.
I hope you drive with the windows down and let the wind rustle through your hair.
I hope you hug.
I hope you kiss.
I hope you surround yourself with people who make you feel alive.
I hope you become a person who brings good energy wherever you go and a person people want to be around.
I hope you speak what's on your mind, that you raise your voice for justice, for peace, for harmony, that you tell others that you love them, before it's too late.
I hope you live louder, live bigger, shine brighter, from this moment on.

Marissa Donnelly

SUNDAY 5

Venture into the great outdoors

APRIL

> Don't be too timid and squeamish about your actions. All life is an experiment. The more experiments you make the better.
>
> *Ralph Waldo Emerson*

MONDAY 6

Join a creative writing group

TUESDAY 7

Don't be limited by the opinions of others

WEDNESDAY 8

Find something to be grateful for

THURSDAY 9

Challenge the conventional

> It takes less time to do a thing right than to explain why you did it wrong.
> Henry Wadsworth Longfellow

FRIDAY 10
Good Friday

You have just one life; this one

SATURDAY 11

Be courageous enough to risk it

SUNDAY 12
Easter Sunday

Follow your own authority

> *If adventure has a final and all-embracing motive, it is surely this: we go out because it is our nature to go out, to climb mountains, and to paddle rivers, to fly to the planets and plunge into the depths of the oceans... When man ceases to do these things, he is no longer man.*
> Wilfrid Noyce

APRIL

Accept responsibility for your life. Know that it is you who will get you where you want to go, no one else.

Les Brown

MONDAY 13
Easter Monday, Bank Holiday

Stay connected

TUESDAY 14

Enrol in an art class

WEDNESDAY 15

Expand your vision of what's possible

THURSDAY 16

It's not all about money

> Don't say you don't have enough time. You have exactly the same number of hours per day that were given to Helen Keller, Pasteur, Michelangelo, Mother Teresa, Leonardo da Vinci, Thomas Jefferson, and Albert Einstein.
>
> *H Jackson Brown Jr*

FRIDAY 17

Don't get too comfortable in your comfort zone

SATURDAY 18

Always come from your heart

SUNDAY 19

Stay true to your values

> If I had asked people what they wanted, they would have said 'faster horses.'
>
> *Henry Ford*

APRIL

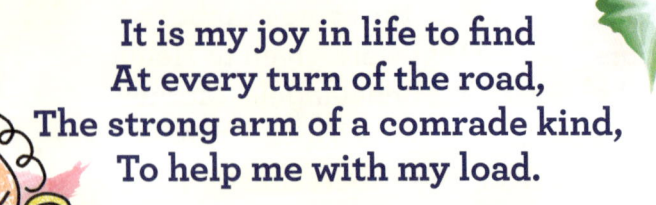

It is my joy in life to find
At every turn of the road,
The strong arm of a comrade kind,
To help me with my load.

And since I have no gold to give
And love alone must make amends,
My only prayer is while I live
"Make me worthy of my friends!"

MONDAY 20

Choose to spend time with people who lift you up

TUESDAY 21

Aim for the win-win outcome

WEDNESDAY 22

Let your energy energise others

> I've been making a list of the things they don't teach you at school. They don't teach you how to love somebody. They don't teach you how to be famous. They don't teach you how to be rich or how to be poor. They don't teach you how to walk away from someone you don't love any longer. They don't teach you how to know what's going on in someone else's mind. They don't teach you what to say when someone is dying. They don't teach you anything worth knowing.
>
> *Neil Gaiman*

THURSDAY 23

Encourage others

FRIDAY 24

Multiple points of view add to the whole picture

SATURDAY 25

Acknowledge your friends

SUNDAY 26

Be kind

APRIL

Make it a rule of life never to regret and never to look back.

Katherine Mansfield

MONDAY 27

Your presence is a gift to the world

TUESDAY 28

Start the day with gratitude

WEDNESDAY 29

Eat nourishing meals

THURSDAY 30

Practice mindfulness

Realise that everything connects to everything else.

Leonardo DaVinci

spriocanna
GOALS
BEALTAINE
MAY

Is ait an mac an saol.
Life is strange.

Aithníonn ciaróg ciaróg eile.
It takes one to know one.

FRIDAY **1**

Explore your creative side

MAY

SATURDAY 2

Plan a family gathering

SUNDAY 3

Aspire to inspire

The words that enlighten the soul are more precious than jewels.

Hazrat Inayat Khan

You must take personal responsibility.
You cannot change the circumstances, the seasons,
or the wind, but you can change yourself.
That is something you have charge of.

Jim Rohn

Be creative

The world as we have created
is a product of our thinking.
It cannot be changed without
changing our thinking.

Albert Einstein

You get in life what you have the courage to ask for.

Oprah Winfrey

MONDAY 4
Bank holiday

Organise a spontaneous get together with friends

BE A FRIEND

Be a friend. You don't need money:
Just a disposition sunny;
Just the wish to help another
Get along some way or other;
Just a kindly hand extended
Out to one who's un-befriended;

Just the will to give or lend,
This will make you someone's friend.

Be a friend. You don't need glory.
Friendship is a simple story.
Pass by trifling errors blindly,
Gaze on honest effort kindly.

Cheer the youth who's bravely trying,
Pity him who's sadly sighing;
Just a little labour spend
On the duties of a friend.

Be a friend. The pay is bigger
(Though not written by a figure)
Than is earned by people clever
In what's merely self-endeavour.

You'll have friends instead of neighbours
For the profits of your labours;
You'll be richer in the end
Than a prince, if you're a friend.

Edgar A Guest

TUESDAY 5

Connect with a like-minded community

If roses grow in heaven, Lord, please pick a bunch for me.
Place them in my mother's arms and tell her they're from me.
Tell her I love and miss her, and when she turns to smile,
Place a kiss upon her cheek and hold her for a while.
Remembering her is easy, I do it every day.
But there's still an ache within my heart
That will never go away.

WEDNESDAY 6

Everything will be alright

THURSDAY 7

Join a walking group

FRIDAY 8

You are known by the company you keep

MAY

> The beginning is the most important part of the work.
> *Plato*

> *We are built to conquer our environment, solve problems and achieve goals. We find no happiness or satisfaction in life without obstacles to overcome and goals to realise.*

> The one thing I'm clear about is everyone is capable of being great. Not compared to someone else. I mean great for yourself.
> *Werner Erhard*

SATURDAY 9

People do what they do

SUNDAY 10

When the going gets tough, keep going

MAY

Many of us crucify ourselves between two thieves — regret for the past and fear of the future.

Fulton Oursler

Everyone thinks of changing the world, but no one thinks of changing himself.

Leo Tolstoy

MONDAY 11

Take the advice you give to others

TUESDAY 12

Do or say something to brighten someone's day

WEDNESDAY 13

Make an impact

THURSDAY 14

Show up, step up, give back.

Lives of great men all remind us
We can make our lives sublime
And departing leave behind us
Footprints on the sands of time.

Footprints that perhaps another
Sailing o'er life's solemn main
A forlorn and shipwrecked brother
Seeing shall take heart again.

Henry Wadsworth Longfellow

FRIDAY 15

Be excited about your life

SATURDAY 16

Patience, persistence and perseverance will get you anywhere

SUNDAY 17

Every expert was once a beginner

Want of care does us more damage than want of knowledge.

Benjamin Franklin

MAY

Beauty is not in the face; beauty is a light in the heart.

Kahlil Gibran

Do what you can, with what you have, where you are.

Theodore Roosevelt

MONDAY 18

What are you ignoring?

TUESDAY 19

The secret is to start before you are ready

WEDNESDAY 20

It always seems impossible until it's done

> **Though we travel the world over to find the beautiful, we must carry it with us or we find it not.**
>
> *Ralph Waldo Emerson*

THURSDAY 21

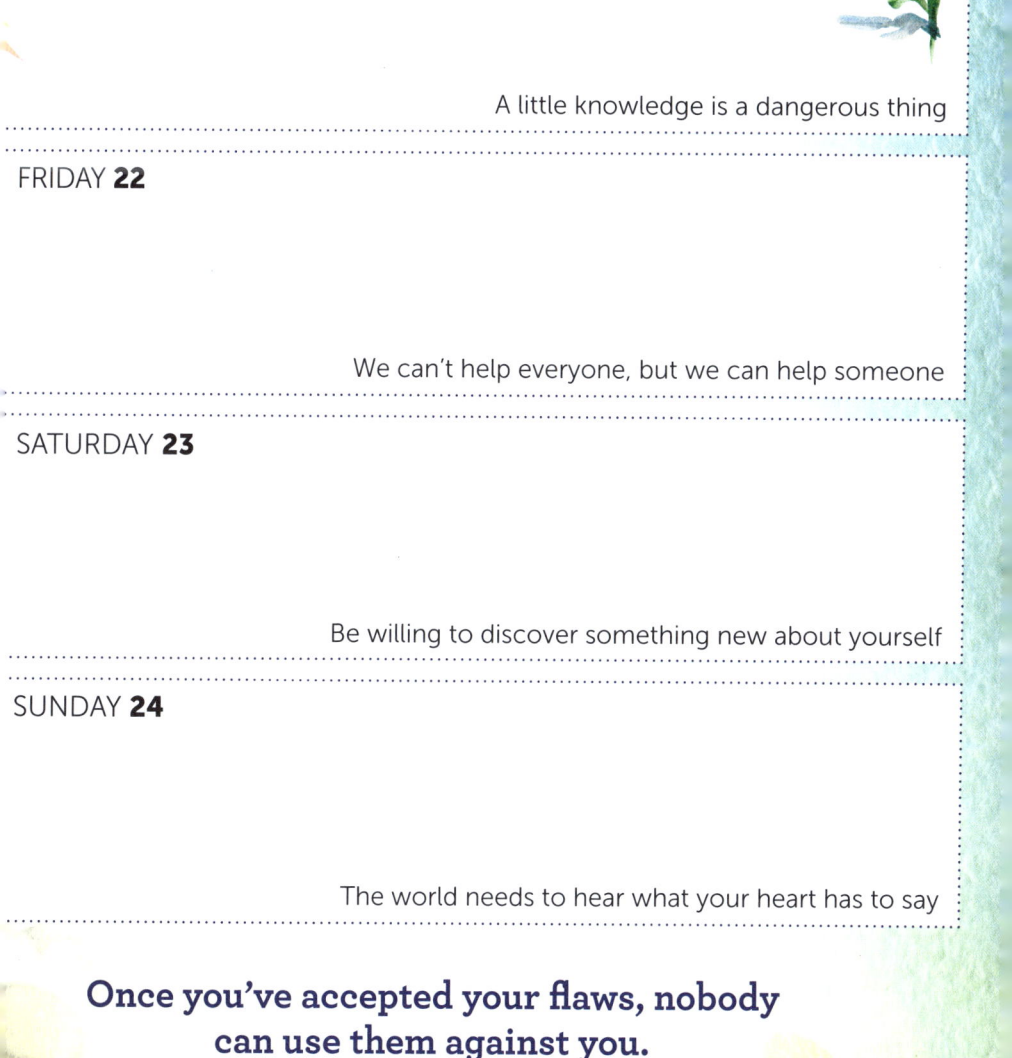

A little knowledge is a dangerous thing

FRIDAY 22

We can't help everyone, but we can help someone

SATURDAY 23

Be willing to discover something new about yourself

SUNDAY 24

The world needs to hear what your heart has to say

> **Once you've accepted your flaws, nobody can use them against you.**
>
> *Game of Thrones*

MAY

> I've got a great ambition to die of exhaustion rather than boredom.
> *Thomas Carlyle*

MONDAY 25

Be your own life coach

TUESDAY 26

Listen generously to others

WEDNESDAY 27

Perfection is a myth

> We must be silent before we can listen.
> We must listen before we can learn.
> We must learn before we can prepare.
> We must prepare before we can serve.
> We must serve before we can lead.
> *William Arthur Ward*

The purpose of life is not to win. The purpose of life is to grow and to share. When you come to look back on all that you have done in life, you will get more satisfaction from the pleasure you have brought into other people's lives than you will from the times that you outdid and defeated them.

Rabbi Harold Kushner

THURSDAY **28**

Agree to disagree or agree on a compromise.

FRIDAY **29**

Life is unpredictable

**Always remember to forget
The things that made you sad,
But never forget to remember
The things that made you glad.**

**Always remember to forget
The troubles that have passed away,
But never, ever forget to remember
The blessings that come each day.**

MAY

It's not your back that hurts;
it's the burden you carry alone.
It's not your eyes that hurt; it's injustice you see.
It's not your ears that hurt; it's the lies you hear.
It's not your head that hurts;
it's the thoughts that torment you.
It's not your lungs that hurt;
it's the breath of change you resist.
It's not your throat that hurts;
it's what you don't express.
It's not your stomach that hurts;
it's what the soul does not digest.
It's not your liver that hurts;
it's the anger you don't forgive.
It's not your heart that hurts;
it's the love in your heart that's not shared.
And it is love itself, for you yourself,
that's the most powerful healer of all.

Author unknown

SATURDAY 30

Make your life your masterpiece

SUNDAY 31

New beginnings are often disguised as painful endings

spriocanna
GOALS

MEITHEAMH
JUNE

_____
_____
_____
_____
_____
_____
_____
_____

Ní thagann ciall roimh aois.
Sense does not come before age.

May good and faithful friends be yours, wherever you may roam.

An rud is annamh is iontach.
What's seldom is wonderful.

JUNE

GOOD IDEA!

Everyone says forgiveness is a lovely idea, until they have something to forgive.
CS Lewis

The price of anything is the amount of life you exchange for it.
Henry David Thoreau

MONDAY 1
Bank holiday

Nothing can bring you peace but yourself

TUESDAY 2

Discover the joy of solitude

WEDNESDAY 3

Do not make yourself indispensable

THURSDAY 4

Live up to your own standards

This is the true joy in life, the being used for a purpose recognised by yourself as a mighty one; the being a force of nature instead of a feverish, selfish little clod of ailments and grievances complaining that the world will not devote itself to making you happy.

I am of the opinion that my life belongs to the whole community, and as long as I live it is my privilege to do for it what I can. I want to be thoroughly used up when I die, for the harder I work the more I live. I rejoice in life for its own sake.

Life is no 'brief candle' for me. It is a sort of splendid torch which I have got hold of for the moment, and I want to make it burn as brightly as possible before handing it on to future generations.

George Bernard Shaw

A loud voice can make even the truth sound foolish.

We need to regularly stop and take stock; to sit down and determine within ourselves which things are worth valuing and which things are not; which risks are worth the cost and which are not.

Epictetus

JUNE

HELP YOURSELF TO HAPPINESS

Everybody, everywhere seeks happiness, it's true,
But finding it and keeping it seem difficult to do.
Difficult because we think that happiness is found
Only in the places where wealth and fame abound.
And so we go on searching in palaces of pleasure
Seeking recognition and monetary treasure,
Unaware that happiness is just a state of mind
Within the reach of everyone who takes time to be kind.
For in making others happy we will be happy, too.
For the happiness you give away returns to shine on you.

Helen Steiner Rice

There are two ways of spreading light; to be the candle or the mirror that reflects it.

Edith Wharton

HUG O' WAR

I will not play at tug o' war.
I'd rather play at hug o' war,
Where everyone hugs
Instead of tugs,
Where everyone giggles
And rolls on the rug,
Where everyone kisses,
And everyone grins,
And everyone cuddles,
And everyone wins.

Shel Silverstein

Your attitude, not your aptitude,
will determine your altitude.

Zig Ziglar

Although no one can go back and make a new start, anyone can start from now and make a new ending.
Mary Robinson

FRIDAY 5

To get going, stop talking and start doing

SATURDAY 6

Remember fondly those you loved and lost

SUNDAY 7

Carry beauty in your eyes and you will see it everywhere

For the great enemy of truth is very often not the lie – the deliberate, contrived and dishonest – but the myth – persistent, persuasive and unrealistic. Too often we hold fast to the clichés of our forebears. We subject all facts to a prefabricated set of interpretations. We enjoy the comfort of opinion over the discomfort of thought.
John F Kennedy

JUNE

MONDAY 8

Time will tell

TUESDAY 9

You can change anything if you care enough

WEDNESDAY 10

Those you judge today will judge you tomorrow

THURSDAY 11

Suspend cynicism

FRIDAY 12

We cannot escape the consequences of our actions

We do not see things as they are, we see things as we are.

Talmud

SATURDAY 13

Leaders don't always lead from the front

SUNDAY 14

The most important thing is to enjoy your life

A tree is known by its fruit; a man by his deeds. A good deed is never lost; he who sows courtesy reaps friendship, and he who plants kindness gathers love.

Saint Basil

Gratitude doesn't change the scenery. It merely washes clean the glass you look through so you can clearly see the colours.

Richelle E Goodrich

When we do the best that we can, we never know what miracle is wrought in our life, or in the life of another.

Helen Keller

Every man is guilty of all the good he didn't do.

Voltaire

JUNE

MONDAY 15

Be a little kinder than necessary

TUESDAY 16

You get in life what you have the courage to ask for

WEDNESDAY 17

Approach new situations with wonder

THURSDAY 18

Be fearless

FRIDAY 19

Direct your anger towards finding solutions

The real voyage of discovery consists not in seeking new landscapes, but in having new eyes.

Marcel Proust

SATURDAY 20

Do what you know is right

SUNDAY 21
Father's Day

In the right light, everything looks beautiful

He never looks for praises.
He's never one to boast.
He just goes on quietly working
For those he loves the most.
His dreams are seldom spoken.
His wants are very few,
And most of the time his worries
Will go unspoken, too.
He's there...a firm foundation
Through all our storms of life,
A sturdy hand to hold onto
In times of stress and strife.
A true friend we can turn to
When times are good or bad.
One of our greatest blessings,
The man that we call Dad.

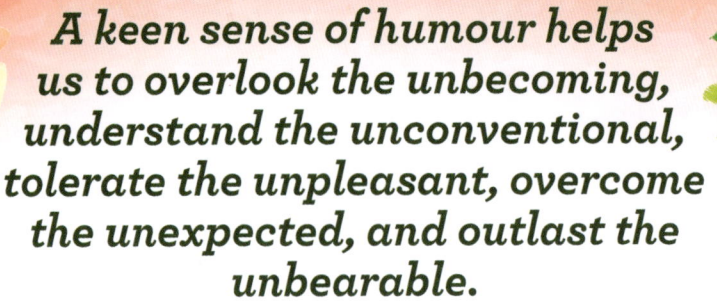

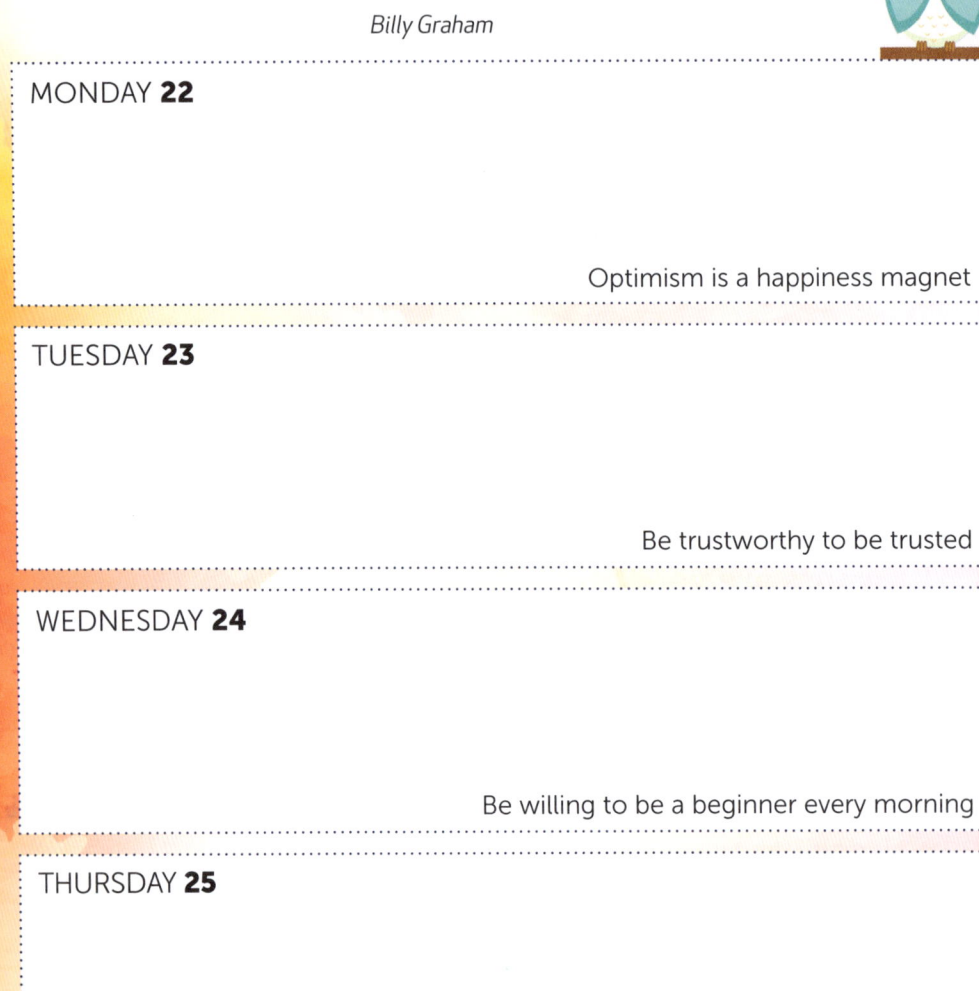

> *A keen sense of humour helps us to overlook the unbecoming, understand the unconventional, tolerate the unpleasant, overcome the unexpected, and outlast the unbearable.*
>
> Billy Graham

MONDAY 22

Optimism is a happiness magnet

TUESDAY 23

Be trustworthy to be trusted

WEDNESDAY 24

Be willing to be a beginner every morning

THURSDAY 25

If you want more luck, take more chances

JUNE

THE HELPING HAND

If when climbing up life's ladder
You can reach a hand below,
Just to help the other fellow
Up another rung or so,
It will be that in the future,
When you're growing weary too,
You'll be glad to find there's someone
Who will lend a hand to you.

FRIDAY 26

Have your words be actions that impact the world

SATURDAY 27

With freedom comes responsibility

SUNDAY 28

A bad penny always turns up

MONDAY 29

Appearances can be deceptive

TUESDAY 30

Bad news travels fast

OPERATING PRINCIPLES FOR A WORLD THAT WORKS FOR EVERYBODY

Respect the other person's point of view, whether or not you agree with it. Recognise that if you had their history, their circumstances, and the forces that play on them, you would likely have their point of view.

Consider life a privilege – all of it, even the parts that are difficult or seem a waste of time. Give up the islands that reinforce mediocrity, the safe places where we gossip and complain to one another, where we are petty.

Take a chance. Be willing to put your reputation on the line; have something at stake.

Work for satisfaction rather than for credit. Keep your word. There will be times when the circumstances of life will make you forget who you are and what you're about. That is when you need to be committed to keeping your word, making what you say count.

Werner Erhard

spriocanna
GOALS
IÚIL
JULY

Tús maith leath na hoibre.
A good start is half the work.

An té a bhíonn siúlach, bíonn scéalach.
He who travels has stories to tell.

WEDNESDAY 1

Don't complain about what you permit

JULY

The purpose of life is not to be happy. It is to be useful, to be honorable, to be compassionate, to have it make some difference that you have lived and lived well.

Ralph Waldo Emerson

God gave us the gift of life; it is up to us to give ourselves the gift of living well.

Voltaire

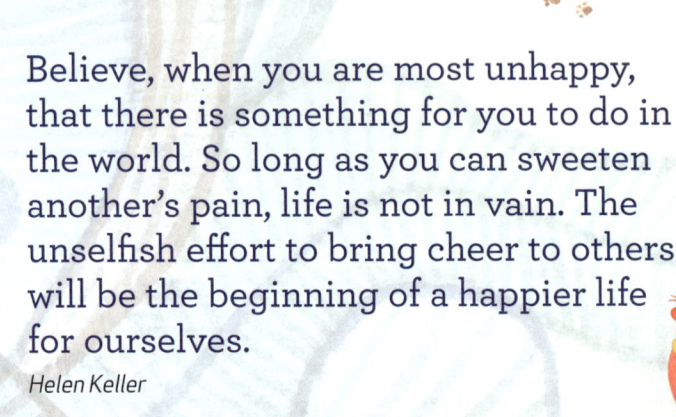

Believe, when you are most unhappy, that there is something for you to do in the world. So long as you can sweeten another's pain, life is not in vain. The unselfish effort to bring cheer to others will be the beginning of a happier life for ourselves.

Helen Keller

THURSDAY 2

Plan for a better world

FRIDAY 3

The faraway hills are not greener

Folks are usually about as happy as they make their minds up to be.

Abraham Lincoln

Language has created the word 'loneliness' to express the pain of being alone. And it has created the word 'solitude' to express the glory of being alone.

Paul Tillich

Not all wounds are visible. Walk gently in the lives of others.

Eleanor Roosevelt

SATURDAY **4**

Every little helps

SUNDAY **5**

Accept that invitation

JULY

MONDAY 6

Take action on fulfilling your dreams

> We must develop and maintain the capacity to forgive. He who is devoid of the power to forgive is devoid of the power to love. There is some good in the worst of us and some evil in the best of us. When we discover this, we are less prone to hate our enemies.
>
> *Martin Luther King Jr*

TUESDAY 7

Go the extra mile

WEDNESDAY 8

If something is worth doing, it's worth doing well

Blessed are the curious for they shall have adventures.

Lovelle Drachman

You cannot get through a single day without impacting the world around you. What you do makes a difference and you have to decide what kind of difference you want to make.

Dr Jane Goodall

THURSDAY 9

Into every life a little rain must fall

FRIDAY 10

Laughter is wonderful medicine

SATURDAY 11

Nothing ventured, nothing gained

SUNDAY 12

Practice what you preach

JULY

Forgiveness is a decision. It's not a feeling, it is a choice.

MONDAY **13**

Seeing is believing

TUESDAY **14**

Make that call

WEDNESDAY **15**

Remember to write thank you notes

THURSDAY **16**

Memorise a favoured poem

Anger ventilated often hurries toward forgiveness; and concealed often hardens into revenge.

Edward G Bulwer-Lytton

> My actions are my only true belongings. I cannot escape the consequences of my actions. My actions are the ground upon which I stand.
> *Thich Nhat Hanh*

FRIDAY 17

See the good in everybody

SATURDAY 18

If you're bored, do something

SUNDAY 19

There is wisdom in unlearning

> We all have our time machines. Some take us back, they're called memories. Some take us forward, they're called dreams.
> *Jeremy Irons*

FOLLOW YOUR DREAMS

> A head full of fears has no space for dreams.
> *Unknown*

JULY

Always be a little kinder than necessary.
James M Barrie

MONDAY 20

Stretch beyond what is comfortable

Beauty is not in the face; beauty is a light in the heart.
Kahlil Gibran

The world is changed by your example, not your opinion.
Paulo Coelho

Anybody can sympathise with the sufferings of a friend, but it requires a very fine nature to sympathise with a friend's success.
Oscar Wilde

Raise your word, not your voice. It is rain that grows flowers, not thunder.
Rumi

TUESDAY 21

Have a sense of humour

> **We are continually faced with great opportunities which are brilliantly disguised as unsolvable problems.**
> *Margaret Mead*

WEDNESDAY 22

People can surprise you

THURSDAY 23

How you say it is as important as what you say

FRIDAY 24

Gardening is cheaper than therapy

SATURDAY 25

Keep your travel kit packed and ready

SUNDAY 26

The quieter you become the more you can hear

> Your task is not to seek for love, but merely to seek and find all the barriers within yourself that you have built against it.
>
> *Rumi*

MONDAY 27

Life goes on

TUESDAY 28

Your will is always within your power

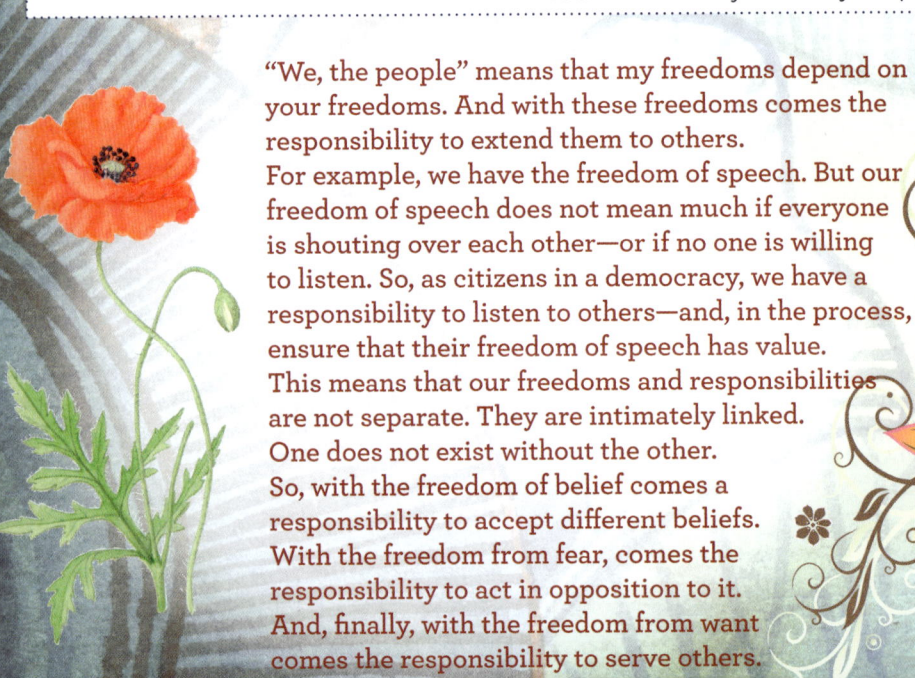

"We, the people" means that my freedoms depend on your freedoms. And with these freedoms comes the responsibility to extend them to others.
For example, we have the freedom of speech. But our freedom of speech does not mean much if everyone is shouting over each other—or if no one is willing to listen. So, as citizens in a democracy, we have a responsibility to listen to others—and, in the process, ensure that their freedom of speech has value.
This means that our freedoms and responsibilities are not separate. They are intimately linked. One does not exist without the other.
So, with the freedom of belief comes a responsibility to accept different beliefs. With the freedom from fear, comes the responsibility to act in opposition to it. And, finally, with the freedom from want comes the responsibility to serve others.

JULY

One must care about a world one will never see.
Bertrand Russell

WEDNESDAY 29

Give more time to yourself

THURSDAY 30

Humour is the best ice breaker

FRIDAY 31

Fear less, trust more

Simplicity, patience, compassion. These three are your greatest treasures. Simple in actions and thoughts, you return to the source of being. Patient with both friends and enemies, you accord with the way things are. Compassionate toward yourself, you reconcile all beings in the world.
Lao Tzu

spriocanna
GOALS
LÚNASA
AUGUST

Take the world nice and easy, and the world will take you the same.

Dá fhada an lá tagann an oíche.
No matter how long the day, the night comes.

Bíonn adharca fada ar na ba thar lear.
Cattle in faraway lands have long horns.

Our lives begin to end the day we become silent about things that matter.
Martin Luther King Jr

We can only be said to be alive in those moments when our hearts are conscious of our treasures.
Thornton Wilder

Bad things do happen; how I respond to them defines my character and the quality of my life. I can choose to sit in perpetual sadness, immobilised by the gravity of my loss, or I can choose to rise from the pain and treasure the most precious gift I have – life itself.
Walter Anderson

Time is what we want most, but what we use worst.
William Penn

SATURDAY 1

Observe nature unfolding

SUNDAY 2

Remember your grandparent's advice

THE INVITATION

It doesn't interest me what you do for a living.
I want to know what you ache for and if you dare
to dream of meeting your heart's longing.

It doesn't interest me how old you are. I want to know
if you will risk looking like a fool for love, for your dream,
for the adventure of being alive.

It doesn't interest me what planets are squaring your moon. I want to know if you have touched the centre of your own sorrow, if you have been opened by life's betrayals or have become shrivelled and closed from fear and further pain. I want to know if you can sit with pain, mine or your own, without moving to hide it or fade it or fix it. I want to know if you can be with joy, mine or your own, if you can dance with wildness and let ecstasy fill you to the tips of your fingers and toes without cautioning us to be careful, to be realistic, to remember the limitations of being human.

It doesn't interest me if the story you are telling is true. I want to know if you can disappoint another to be true to yourself; if you can bear the accusation of betrayal and not betray your own soul; if you can be faithless and therefore trustworthy. I want to know if you can see beauty even when it's not pretty, every day. And if you can source your own life from its presence. I want to know if you can live with failure, yours and mine, and still stand on the edge of the lake and shout to the silver of the moon "Yes.".

It doesn't interest me to know where you live or how much money you have. I want to know if you can get up, after the night of grief and despair, weary and bruised to the bone, and do what needs to be done to feed the children. It doesn't interest me who you know or how you came to be here. I want to know if you will stand in the centre of the fire with me and not shrink back.

It doesn't interest me where or what or with whom you have studied. I want to know what sustains you from the inside when all else falls away. I want to know if you can be alone with yourself and if you truly like the company you keep in the empty moments.

Oriah Mountain Dreamer

AUGUST

The world has enough beautiful mountains and meadows, spectacular skies and serene lakes. It has enough lush forests, flowered fields, and sandy beaches. It has plenty of stars and the promise of a new sunrise and sunset every day. What the world needs more of is people to appreciate and enjoy it.

Michael Josephson

MONDAY 3
Bank holiday

Resist the urge to gossip

TUESDAY 4

Tackle your problems head on

Be the master of your destiny, not a victim of your history.

AUGUST

Life is amazing. And then it's awful. And then it's amazing again. And in between the amazing and the awful, it's ordinary and mundane and routine. Breathe in the amazing, hold on through the awful, and relax and exhale through the ordinary. That's just living a heartbreaking, soul healing, amazing, awful, ordinary life. And it's breathtakingly beautiful.

LR Knost

At times our own light goes out and is rekindled by a spark from another person. Each of us has cause to think with deep gratitude of those who have lighted the flame within us.

Albert Schweitzer

WEDNESDAY 5

A good deed is never lost

THURSDAY 6

Ditch the 'cudda, wudda, shudda' sisters

> **Time** ripens all things;
> with **time** all things are revealed;
> **time** is the father of **truth**.
>
> *Francois Rabelais*

FRIDAY 7

Confirm all appointments

SATURDAY 8

Play your cards right

> ## Let us be grateful to people who make us happy.
>
> *Marcel Proust*

> Appreciation is a wonderful thing.
> It makes what is excellent in others
> belong to us as well.
>
> *Voltaire*

SUNDAY 9

Creative thinking is inspired by limited resources

AUGUST

*May brooks and trees and singing hills
join in the chorus too,
and every gentle wind that blows
send happiness to you.*

MONDAY 10

Be a good loser and a good winner

TUESDAY 11

Know that life is all about the unknown

WEDNESDAY 12

You are never too wise to learn

THURSDAY 13

Enjoy the occasion

I can shake off everything as I write; my sorrows disappear, my courage is reborn.

Anne Frank

FRIDAY 14

There is no time like the present

SATURDAY 15

Be kind to yourself

What seeds have you been planting
In the garden of your heart?
What will be forthcoming
When the germination starts?
If gracious thoughts are planted,
The returns will surely be
A harvest full of beauty,
Which you will plainly see.
If your thoughts are dark and dreary,
You are very apt to find
That weeds will soon be growing –
The most depressing kind.

SUNDAY 16

Listening matters

AUGUST

Nothing is so fatiguing as the eternal hanging on of an uncompleted task.
William James

MONDAY 17

We are shaped and fashioned by what we love

TUESDAY 18

Every possession implies a duty

WEDNESDAY 19

We give life meaning

Be not afraid of life. Believe that life is worth living, and your belief will help create the fact.
Henry James

Life is a progress, and not a station.
Ralph Waldo Emerson

THURSDAY 20

Be slow to judge

> *When I run after what I think I want,*
> *my days are a furnace of distress and anxiety.*
> *If I sit in my own place of patience,*
> *what I need flows to me, without pain.*
> *From this, I understand that what I want*
> *also wants me, is looking for me*
> *and attracting me.*
>
> Rumi

FRIDAY 21

Remain calm in the storm

SATURDAY 22

Travel through life with a rich soul

SUNDAY 23

Miracles do happen

Wherever you go, go with all your heart.
Confucius

Many of life's failures are people who did not realise how close they were to success when they gave up.
Thomas Edison

MONDAY 24

Choose your battles wisely

TUESDAY 25

Have pleasure in giving pleasure

WEDNESDAY 26

Stretch your mind

THURSDAY 27

Ask better questions

AUGUST

In the mind of the expert there are very few possibilities, but in the Beginner's Mind there are infinite possibilities because we come to it fresh. So it is a kind of a discipline to try to bring Beginners Mind to every aspect of life and not be so stuck in our ideas and opinions.

Jon Kabat Zinn

But let there be spaces in your togetherness and let the winds of the heavens dance between you. Love one another but make not a bond of love: let it rather be a moving sea between the shores of your souls.

Khalil Gibran

FRIDAY 28

Conquering fear is the beginning of wisdom

SATURDAY 29

Speak with dignity

SUNDAY 30

Give people the benefit of the doubt

We are free to choose, but we are not free from the consequences of our choice.

MONDAY 31

It takes two to start an argument

Life is an echo. What you send out, comes back. What you sow, you reap. What you give, you get. What you see in others, exists in you.

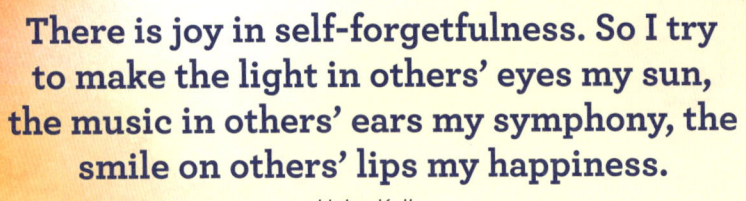

There is joy in self-forgetfulness. So I try to make the light in others' eyes my sun, the music in others' ears my symphony, the smile on others' lips my happiness.

Helen Keller

If in our daily life we can smile, if we can be peaceful and happy, not only we, but everyone will profit from it. This is the most basic kind of peace work.

Thich Nhat Hanh

spriocanna
GOALS
MEÁN FOMHAIR
SEPTEMBER

Fall Brings New Hope

May love and laughter light your days, and warm your heart and home.

Is olc an ghaoth nach séideann do dhuine éigin.

It's an ill wind that doesn't blow someone some good.

TUESDAY 1

Flow with nature, not against her

SEPTEMBER

GET UP AND GO

How do I know my youth has been spent?
Because my get-up-and-go, got up and went.
But in spite of all that, I'm able to grin
When I think where my get-up-and-go has been.

Old age is golden, I've heard it said,
But sometimes I wonder as I go to bed –
My ears in a drawer, my teeth in a cup,
My eyes on a table until I wake up.

When I was young my slippers were red,
I could kick my heels right over my head.
When I grew older my slippers were blue,
But I could still dance the whole night thru.

Now that I am old my slippers are black,
I walk to the corner and puff my way back.
The reason I know my youth is spent,
My get-up-and-go got up and went.

I get up each morning dust off my wits,
Pick up the paper and read the "orbits".
If my name is missing, I know I'm not dead,
So I eat a good breakfast and go back to bed.

Pete Seeger

Nothing is a waste of time if you use the experience wisely.
Auguste Rodin

We need limitations and temptations to open our inner selves, dispel our ignorance, tear off disguises, throw down old idols, and destroy false standards. Only by such rude awakenings can we be led to dwell in a place where we are less cramped, less hindered by the ever-insistent external. Only then do we discover a new capacity and appreciation of goodness and beauty and truth.

Helen Keller

WEDNESDAY 2

Everybody is perfectly imperfect

THURSDAY 3

Walk confidently towards the future

What seem to us as bitter trials are often blessings in disguise.

Oscar Wilde

SEPTEMBER

I will love the sun for it warms my bones;
Yet I will love the rain for it cleanses my spirit.
I will love the light for it shows me the way;
Yet I will love the darkness for it shows me the stars.
I will welcome happiness for it enlarges my heart;
Yet I will endure sadness for it opens my soul.
I will acknowledge rewards for they are my due;
Yet I will welcome obstacles for they are my challenge

Randy Morgenson

FRIDAY 4

Enjoy other people enjoying life

SATURDAY 5

Lift people up

SUNDAY 6

Do not delay; golden moments fly by

Hot heads and cold hearts never solved anything.

Billy Graham

MONDAY **7**

A debt is cheaper if paid quickly

TUESDAY **8**

We only know what we think we know

WEDNESDAY **9**

Never cut what can be untied

THURSDAY **10**

Get enough sleep

FRIDAY **11**

Who ever gossips to you will gossip about you

SEPTEMBER

DRY YOUR TEARS

You can shed tears that she is gone, or you can smile because she has lived.
You can close your eyes and pray that she'll come back, or you can open your eyes and see all she's left.
Your heart can be empty because you can't see her, or you can be full of the love you shared.
You can turn your back on tomorrow and live yesterday, or you can be happy for tomorrow because of yesterday.
You can remember her and only that she's gone, or you can cherish her memory and let it live on.
You can cry and close your mind, be empty and turn your back, or you can do what she'd want: smile, open your eyes, love and go on.

David Harkins

SATURDAY 12

When life speeds up, slow down

SUNDAY 13

Accentuate the positive

MONDAY 14

Take a chance!

TUESDAY 15

Good health is true wealth

CARETAKE THIS MOMENT

Immerse yourself in its particulars. Respond to this person, this challenge, this deed. Quit the evasions. Stop giving yourself needless trouble.

It is time to really live; to fully inhabit the situation you happen to be in now. You are not some disinterested bystander. Exert yourself.

Respect your partnership with providence. Ask yourself often – how may I perform this particular deed such that it would be consistent with and acceptable to the divine will? Heed the answer and get to work.

When your doors are shut and your room is dark you are not alone. The will of nature is within you as your natural genius is within. Listen to its importunings. Follow its directives.

As concerns the art of living, the material is your own life. No great thing is created suddenly. There must be time.

Give your best and always be kind.
Epictetus

WEDNESDAY 16

Friendship has no rules

SEPTEMBER

> All men dream, but not equally. Those who dream by night in the dusty recesses of their minds, wake in the day to find that it was vanity: but the dreamers of the day are dangerous men, for they may act on their dreams with open eyes, to make them possible.
>
> *TE Lawrence*

THURSDAY **17**

Too much love is never enough

FRIDAY **18**

Leave everything a little better than you found it

SATURDAY **19**

You can do a lot in one day

SUNDAY **20**

Everything is relative

It is wise to direct your anger towards problems – not people; to focus your energies on answers – not excuses.

William Arthur Ward

MONDAY 21

Make happiness a habit

TUESDAY 22

Character is revealed in moments of challenge

WEDNESDAY 23

Life itself tends to explain life itself

The conditions are never right. People who delay action until all factors are favourable – do nothing.

Life is a gift, and it offers us the privilege, opportunity, and responsibility to give something back by becoming more.

Tony Robbins

SEPTEMBER

> There are those who look at things
> the way they are, and ask why?
> I dream of things that never were
> and ask why not?
>
> *George Bernard Shaw*

THURSDAY 24

Procrastination is the thief of dreams

FRIDAY 25

Take the opportunity to express love

SATURDAY 26

Talk about more than the weather

SUNDAY 27

Ask your purse what you should buy

The world is changed by your example, not your opinion.
Paul Coelho

Anyone who keeps the ability to see beauty never grows old.
Franz Kafka

MONDAY 28

Make a secret wish

TUESDAY 29

Do the most difficult task first

WEDNESDAY 30

Now is the best time to begin

If we really want to love, we must learn how to forgive.
Mother Teresa

spriocanna GOALS

DEIREADH FOMHAIR
OCTOBER

A little fire that warms is better than a big fire that burns.

Ní neart go cur le chéile.
There's strength in unity.

THURSDAY 1

There's a story worth telling in everyone's life

FRIDAY 2

Heroes have flaws too

THE POWER OF ONE

One song can spark a moment,
One flower can wake the dream.
One tree can start a forest,
One bird can herald spring.
One smile begins a friendship,
One handclasp lifts a soul.
One star can guide a ship at sea,
One word can frame the goal.
One vote can change a nation,
One sunbeam lights a room.
One candle wipes out darkness,
One laugh will conquer gloom.
One step must start each journey,
One word must start each prayer.
One hope will raise our spirits,
One touch can show you care.
One voice can speak with wisdom,
One heart can know what's true.
One life can make a difference.
You see, it's up to you!

SATURDAY 3

The nature of things does not change

SUNDAY 4

Make full use of what happens to you

OCTOBER

I went to the woods because I wished to live deliberately, to front only the essential facts of life, and see if I could not learn what it had to teach, and not, when I came to die, discover that I had not lived. I did not wish to live what was not life, living is so dear; nor did I wish to practice resignation, unless it was quite necessary. I wanted to live deep and suck out all the marrow of life, to live so sturdily and Spartan-like as to put to rout all that was not life, to cut a broad swath and shave close, to drive life into a corner, and reduce it to its lowest terms.

Henry David Thoreau

There is no one living who isn't capable of doing more than he thinks he can do.

Henry Ford

As we express our gratitude, we must never forget that the highest appreciation is not to utter words, but to live by them.

John F Kennedy

> **What's going on in the inside shows on the outside.**
> *Earl Nightingale*

MONDAY 5

Dreams are a place to escape to

> **The happiness of your life depends upon the quality of your thoughts.**
> *Marcus Aurelius*

TUESDAY 6

Success rarely comes without a struggle

WEDNESDAY 7

Adversity is never boring

THURSDAY 8

The time to be happy is now

OCTOBER

> He is richest who is content with the least, for contentment is the wealth of nature.
> *Socrates*

> If there is any one secret of success, it lies in the ability to get the other person's point of view and see things from that person's angle as well as from your own.
> Henry Ford

FRIDAY 9

Face what you fear

SATURDAY 10

Where do you want to go today?

SUNDAY 11

Smile as much as you can

MONDAY 12

Face up to your responsibilities

> **You can't build a reputation on what you are going to do.**
> *Henry Ford*

TUESDAY 13

Think big

WEDNESDAY 14

Be brave enough to say "I don't know"

THURSDAY 15

Get out of your own way

FRIDAY 16

Desire keeps the economy going

OCTOBER

DESIGN YOUR FREE TIME

Don't over schedule.
Engage in unstructured sports and activities – it's called play!
Be spontaneous – interesting stuff might happen.
Have frequent conversations about nothing in particular.
Have one family meal per day – get to know each other
as you grow up around the table.
Engage with real people – over coffee, lunch, dinner,
a glass of wine, and learn to relax in company.
Find a good bookshop and practice browsing.
Develop a habit of reading books.
Have digital free time and place zones.
Get enough sleep.

SATURDAY 17

Don't trust your memory – write it down

SUNDAY 18

Stand by your friends

> Wisdom is the reward for
> surviving our own stupidity.
> *Brian Rathbone*

A good life is when you smile often, dream big, laugh a lot and realise how blessed you are for what you have.

MONDAY 19

Find your own life interesting

TUESDAY 20

Bad things happen to good people

WEDNESDAY 21

Don't believe everything you hear (or read)

THURSDAY 22

Acknowledge your past achievements

FRIDAY 23

We are living examples

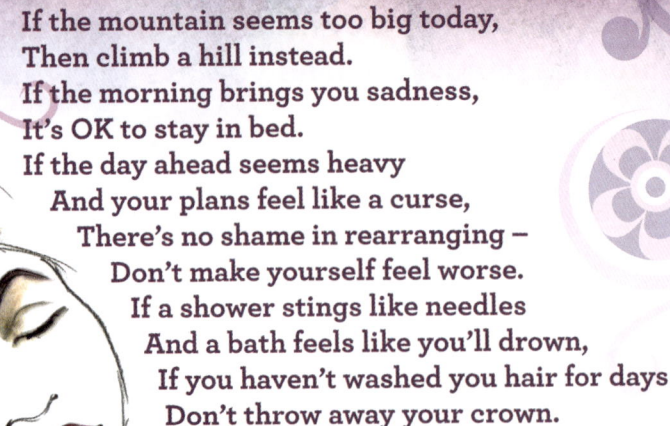

If the mountain seems too big today,
Then climb a hill instead.
If the morning brings you sadness,
It's OK to stay in bed.
If the day ahead seems heavy
  And your plans feel like a curse,
    There's no shame in rearranging –
      Don't make yourself feel worse.
        If a shower stings like needles
          And a bath feels like you'll drown,
            If you haven't washed you hair for days
          Don't throw away your crown.
        A day is not a lifetime,
      A rest is not defeat,
    Don't think if it as failure –
Just a quiet, kind retreat.
It's OK to take a moment
From an anxious fractured mind,
The world will not stop turning
While you get realigned.
The mountain will still be there
when you want to try again.
You can climb it in your own time,
Just love yourself till then.

Laura Ding Edwards

SATURDAY 24

Timing is everything

SUNDAY 25

Meet people where they are

OCTOBER

MONDAY 26
Bank holiday

The world needs leaders and followers

TUESDAY 27

Seeing is believing (unless it's Photoshopped)

WEDNESDAY 28

Expect the unexpected

THURSDAY 29

What's done is done

Peace is the beauty of life. It is sunshine.
It is the smile of a child, the love of a mother,
the joy of a father, the togetherness of a family.
It is the advancement of man, the victory of a
just cause, the triumph of truth.

Menachem Begin

OCTOBER

The marvellous richness of human experience would lose something of rewarding joy if there were no limitations to overcome. The hilltop hour would not be half so wonderful if there were no dark valleys to traverse.

Helen Keller

FRIDAY 30

A clear conscience makes a restful pillow

SATURDAY 31

Mistakes are opportunities to learn

Do not indulge in dreams of having what you have not, but reckon up the chief of the blessings you do possess, and then thankfully remember how you would crave for them if they were not yours.

Marcus Aurelius

Gratitude makes sense of our past, brings peace for today, and creates a vision for tomorrow.

Melody Beattie

spriocanna
GOALS

SAMHAIN
NOVEMBER

All the world's a stage and most of us are desperately unrehearsed.

Ní huasal ná íseal, ach thuas seal is thíos seal.
Neither noble nor lowly, but up for a while and down for a while.

_____
_____
_____
_____
_____
_____
_____
_____

Níl aon tóin tinn mar do thóin tinn féin.
There's no sore ass like your own sore ass.

SUNDAY **1**

Don't betray a confidence

NOVEMBER

> Courage is contagious. When a brave man takes a stand, the spines of others are stiffened.
> *Billy Graham*

MONDAY 2

A little dirt never hurt anyone

TUESDAY 3

An injured friend is the bitterest of foes

WEDNESDAY 4

Humour negates many an upset

THURSDAY 5

Life is a journey of growth and development

> *If you can't explain it simply, you don't understand it well enough.*
> — Albert Einstein

> Gratitude is something of which none of us can give too much. For on the smiles, the thanks we give, our little gestures of appreciation, our neighbours build their philosophy of life.
> — AJ Cronin

> **Wealth consists not in having great possessions, but in having few wants.**
> — *Epicurus*

FRIDAY 6

Pursue more than just pleasure

SATURDAY 7

Choose a mighty purpose for your life

SUNDAY 8

Allow yourself to feel rich without money

NOVEMBER

It isn't what you have in your pocket that makes you thankful, but what you have in your heart.

MONDAY 9

Accept challenges

TUESDAY 10

Be at ease with not knowing and be willing to discover

WEDNESDAY 11

Shared experiences make great conversation

THURSDAY 12

Life is a coin you can spend only once

If we magnified blessings as much as we magnify disappointments, we would all be much happier.
John Wooden

> **To know what is right and not do it is the worst cowardice.**
> *Confucius*

FRIDAY 13

Starting a good book is like setting out on a wonderful journey

10 DAYS OF TRANSFORMATION

DAY 1: Transform your excuses into actions.
DAY 2: Accept 100% responsibility for your life.
DAY 3: Stop playing the blame game.
DAY 4: Celebrate your past accomplishments.
DAY 5: Focus on the one thing you need to change.
DAY 6: Visualise what success looks like for you.
DAY 7: Discover a purpose worthy of your life.
DAY 8: Make room for failure on the road to fulfilment.
DAY 9: Get clear on what you really want.
DAY 10: Commit to bringing your best to the table.

SATURDAY 14

Kindness is the sunshine of life

SUNDAY 15

Refuse to be negative

NOVEMBER

Every action has an equal and opposite reaction. This is a law of the universe and spares none. Wrong done and injustice inflicted is paid back in the same coin. No one has escaped the justice of the universe. It is only a matter of time.

Anil Sinha

MONDAY 16

An apple a day keeps the doctor away

TUESDAY 17

Take advice from those you admire

WEDNESDAY 18

Resist the urge to judge others

As the eagle was killed by the arrow winged with his own feather, so the hand of the world is wounded by its own skill.

Helen Keller

> *The tragedy of life is not that it ends so soon, but that we wait so long to begin it.*
> WM Lewis

THURSDAY 19

Don't believe everything you think

FRIDAY 20

Shame is a poisonous emotion

SATURDAY 21

Accept what you have asked for

SUNDAY 22

Question your prejudices

Today is life – the only life you are sure of. Make the most of today. Get interested in something. Shake yourself awake. Develop a hobby. Let the winds of enthusiasm sweep through you. Live today with gusto.
Dale Carnegie

NOVEMBER

Indifference and neglect often do much more damage than outright dislike.
JK Rowling

MONDAY 23

Live your life at cause, not at effect

TUESDAY 24

Worry is a misuse of your imagination

WEDNESDAY 25

The future arrives every day

People will forget what you said. People will forget what you did, but they will never forget how you made them feel.
Maya Angelou

You really can change the world if you care enough.
Marian Wright Edelman

Abraham Maslow believed that 15 minutes was more than enough to spend on our problems. Whenever a patient would visit Maslow's office, he would allow them to talk about their problems up to 15 minutes and then he would have them focus on the desired outcome. He wanted them to focus most of their time and energy talking about the things they wanted to achieve, on the solutions to their so called problems, not on the problems.

THURSDAY **26**

There is a difference between spending and investing

FRIDAY **27**

Effort brings its own satisfaction

SATURDAY **28**

Don't be stingy with your hugs

SUNDAY **29**

Curl up with a good book

Wisdom is only found in truth.
Goethe

NOVEMBER

THE PARADOXICAL COMMANDMENTS

People are often unreasonable, irrational, and self-centred.
Forgive them anyway.

If you are kind, people may accuse you of selfish, ulterior motives.
Be kind anyway.

If you are successful, you will win some unfaithful friends and some genuine enemies.
Succeed anyway.

If you are honest and sincere people may deceive you.
Be honest and sincere anyway.

What you spend years creating, others could destroy overnight.
Create anyway.

If you find serenity and happiness, some may be jealous.
Be happy anyway.

The good you do today, may be forgotten by them tomorrow.
Do good anyway.

Give the best you have, and it may never be enough.
Give your best anyway.

In the final analysis, it was never between you and them anyway.

Mother Teresa

MONDAY 30

Pay what you owe

CHRISTMAS SHOPPING LIST

1. Buy a 2021 Get Up and Go Diary for all my friends.

2. Buy a Get Up and Go Travel Journal and plan my next trip.

3. Buy a Daily Planner for…

4. Buy a Genius Journal for…

People never learn anything by being told, they have to find out for themselves.
Paulo Coelho

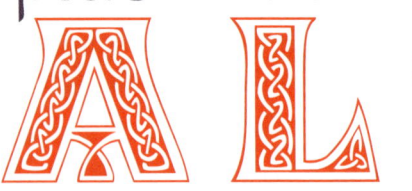

GOALS
spriocanna
NOLLAIG
DECEMBER

_____
_____
_____
_____
_____
_____
_____
_____
_____
_____
_____
_____
_____

Is treise an dúchas ná an oiliúint.
Nature is stronger than nurture.

May all life's passing seasons bring the best to you and yours.

Ní dhéanfadh an saol capall rása d'asal.
Nobody can make a racehorse out of a donkey.

Hello winter

BECAUSE YOU HAVE LIVED

To laugh often and much.
To win the respect of intelligent people,
and the affection of children.
To earn the appreciation of honest critics.
To appreciate beauty.
To find the best in others.
To leave the world a bit better, whether by
a healthy child, or a garden patch.
To know even one life has breathed
easier because you have lived.
This is to have succeeded.

Each morning when I open my eyes I say to myself: I, not events, have the power to make me happy or unhappy today. I can choose which it shall be. Yesterday is dead, tomorrow hasn't arrived yet. I have just one day, today, and I'm going to be happy.

Groucho Marx

TUESDAY **1**

People take you at your word – don't mess with it

DECEMBER

OUR PARENTS

Our parents cast long shadows over our lives. When we grow up we imagine that we can walk into the sun, ahead of them.
We don't realise until it's too late that we have no choice in the matter, they're always ahead of us.
We carry them within us all our lives, in the shape of our face, the way we walk, the sound of our voice, our skin, our hair, our hands, our heart.
We try all our lives to separate ourselves from them and only when they are passed on do we find that we are.
We grow to expect that our parents, like the weather, will always be with us. Then they are gone, leaving a mark like a hand print on wet glass or a kiss on a rainy day, and with their passing we are no longer children.
It is not our job to judge our parents performance. If we can understand that what our parents say is a very imperfect expression of perfect love, our relationship with them will be transformed.

Richard Eyre

WEDNESDAY **2**

Forgive yourself – it will set you free

Courage is like love; it must have hope for nourishment.

Napoleon

THURSDAY 3

Get to know your neighbours

FRIDAY 4

Never lose the desire to play

SATURDAY 5

Listen to your children

SUNDAY 6

Energise yourself

You cannot be lonely if you like the person you're alone with.

Wayne Dyer

DECEMBER

TAKE TIME

Take time to think;
It is the source of power.
Take time to read;
It is the foundation of wisdom.
Take time to play;
It is the secret of staying young.
Take time to be quiet;
It is the opportunity to seek peace.
Take time to be aware;
It is the opportunity to help others.
Take time to laugh;
It is the music of the soul.
Take time to be friendly;
It is the road to happiness.
Take time to dream;
It is what the future is made of.
Take time to love;
It is the greatest power on earth.
There is time for everything.

> The greatest happiness of life is the conviction that we are loved; loved for ourselves, or rather, loved in spite of ourselves.
>
> *Victor Hugo*

MONDAY 7

Ask for support

> **Knowing others is intelligence; knowing yourself is true wisdom. Mastering others is strength; mastering yourself is true power.**
> *Tao Te Ching*

TUESDAY 8

Walk tall, walk straight and look the world right in the eye

I AM

*I know not whence I came,
I know not whither I go;
But the fact stands clear that I am here
In this world of pleasure and woe.
And out of the mist and murk
Another truth shines plain –
It is my power each day and hour
To add to its joy or its pain.*

Ella Wheeler Wilcox

WEDNESDAY 9

Your happiness is up to you

THURSDAY 10

Never believe you are not good enough

DECEMBER

Your pain is the breaking of the shell that encloses your understanding ... and if you could keep your heart in wonder at the daily miracles of life, your pain would not seem less wonderous than your joy.

Khalil Gibran

Instead of comparing our lot with that of those who are more fortunate than we are, we should compare it with the lot of the great majority of our fellow men. It then appears that we are among the privileged.

Helen Keller

FRIDAY 11

Make opportunities for yourself

SATURDAY 12

Do not accept unacceptable behaviour

SUNDAY 13

Find your own philosophy and live life on your terms

It is often in the darkest skies that we see the brightest stars.

Richard Evans

MONDAY 14

Inner direction gives focus and strength

The aim of life is to live, and to live means to be aware, joyously, drunkenly, serenely, divinely aware.

Henry Millar

TUESDAY 15

Allow for unstructured time

WEDNESDAY 16

Discover the joy of your own company

THURSDAY 17

If you want peace, stop doing what annoys you

DECEMBER

Believe. No pessimist ever discovered the secrets of the stars, or sailed to an uncharted island, or opened a new heaven to the human spirit.

Helen Keller

FRIDAY 18

You cannot fake integrity

It is easier to act yourself into a new way of feeling rather than feel your way into a new way of acting.

GD Morgan

**Only as high as I reach can I grow.
Only as far as I see can I go.
Only as much as I live can I be.
Only so much as I do can I know.**

SATURDAY 19

Feelings need expression

SUNDAY 20

Good thoughts are half of good health

> When we are tired, we are attacked by ideas we conquered long ago.
>
> *Friedrich Nietzsche*

MONDAY 21

The less we know the more we suspect

HOW DO YOU LIVE YOUR DASH?

I read of a man who stood to speak at the funeral of a friend.
He referred to the dates on his coffin, from the beginning... to the end.
He noted that first came his date of birth and spoke the following date with tears, but he said what mattered most of all was the dash between those years.
For that dash represents all the time that he spent alive on earth... and now only those who loved him know what that little line is worth.
For it matters not, how much we own; the cars... the house... the cash,
What matters is how we live and love and how we spend our dash.

Linda M Ellis

DECEMBER

TUESDAY 22

Everyone has strengths and weaknesses

Life is full of surprises and unexpected opportunities.

And once the storm is over, you won't remember how you made it through. How you managed to survive. You won't even be sure whether the storm is really over. But one thing is certain. When you come out of the storm, you won't be the same person who walked in. That's what the storm is all about.

Haruki Murakami

WEDNESDAY 23

Words are your most powerful weapon; use with care

THURSDAY 24

Many hands make light work

CHRISTMAS GIFTS

The gifts I'd leave beneath your tree,
Aren't those that you can touch or see,
not wrapped in Christmas tissue gay
but gifts to bless you every day.
The gift of friendship warm and true,
Is one that I would leave for you
Good health and happiness and cheer
to keep you smiling through the year.
The gift of peace that comes from God,
with prayer to guide each path you trod
and when your heart has lost its song
the gift of hope to cheer you on.

Author unknown

FRIDAY 25
Christmas Day

Live life as a joyful contribution

SATURDAY 26

Listen to the laughter of children

SUNDAY 27

Praise twice as much as you criticise

DECEMBER

One of the greatest gifts you can give to anyone is the gift of your attention.
Jim Rohn

MONDAY 28

Forgiving benefits the forgiver and the forgiven

TUESDAY 29

Today is the someday you promised yourself

WEDNESDAY 30

The only life you can live is your own

When you find peace within yourself, you become the kind of person who can live at peace with others.
Peace Pilgrim

THURSDAY 31
New Year's Eve

Hindsight is always 20/20

Life is a series of natural and spontaneous changes. Don't resist them — that only creates sorrow. Let reality be reality. Let things flow naturally forward in whatever way they like.

Lao Tzu

For last year's words belong to last year's language. And next year's words await another voice. And to make an end is to make a beginning.

TS Eliot

A TOAST TO 2021

At the sound of the tolling midnight bell
a brand new year will begin.
Let's raise our hopes in a confidant toast,
to the promise it ushers in.
May your battles be few, your pleasure many,
your wishes and dreams fulfilled.
May your confidence stand in the face of loss
and give you the strength to rebuild.
May peace of heart fill all your days
may serenity grace your soul.
May tranquil moments bless your life
and keep your spirit whole.

DESIDERATA

Go placidly amid the noise and haste, and remember what peace there may be in silence. As far as possible without surrender be on good terms with all persons. Speak your truth quietly and clearly, and listen to others, even the dull and ignorant; they too have their story.

Avoid loud and aggressive persons, they are vexations to the spirit. If you compare yourself with others, you may become vain and bitter; for always there will be greater and lesser persons than yourself. Enjoy your achievements as well as your plans. Keep interested in your own career, however humble; it is a real possession in the changing fortunes of time. Exercise caution in your business affairs; for the world is full of trickery. But let this not blind you to what virtue there is; many persons strive for high ideals; and everywhere life is full of heroism.

Be yourself. Especially, do not feign affection. Neither be cynical about love; for in the face of all aridity and disenchantment it is perennial as the grass. Take kindly the counsel of the years, gracefully surrendering the things of youth. Nurture strength of spirit to shield you in sudden misfortune. But do not distress yourself with imaginings. Many fears are born of fatigue and loneliness. Beyond a wholesome discipline, be gentle with yourself.

You are a child of the universe, no less than the trees and the stars; you have a right to be here. And whether or not it is clear to you, no doubt the universe is unfolding as it should. Therefore be at peace with God, whatever you conceive Him to be; and whatever your labours and aspirations, in the noisy confusion of life keep peace with your soul. With all its sham, drudgery and broken dreams, it is still a beautiful world. Be cheerful. Strive to be happy.

Max Ehrmann

2021 CALENDAR

January
S	M	T	W	T	F	S
					1	2
3	4	5	6	7	8	9
10	11	12	13	14	15	16
17	18	19	20	21	22	23
24	25	26	27	28	29	30
31						

February
S	M	T	W	T	F	S
	1	2	3	4	5	6
7	8	9	10	11	12	13
14	15	16	17	18	19	20
21	22	23	24	25	26	27
28						

March
S	M	T	W	T	F	S
	1	2	3	4	5	6
7	8	9	10	11	12	13
14	15	16	17	18	19	20
21	22	23	24	25	26	27
28	29	30	31			

April
S	M	T	W	T	F	S
				1	2	3
4	5	6	7	8	9	10
11	12	13	14	15	16	17
18	19	20	21	22	23	24
25	26	27	28	29	30	

May
S	M	T	W	T	F	S
						1
2	3	4	5	6	7	8
9	10	11	12	13	14	15
16	17	18	19	20	21	22
23	24	25	26	27	28	29
30	31					

June
S	M	T	W	T	F	S
		1	2	3	4	5
6	7	8	9	10	11	12
13	14	15	16	17	18	19
20	21	22	23	24	25	26
27	28	29	30			

July
S	M	T	W	T	F	S
				1	2	3
4	5	6	7	8	9	10
11	12	13	14	15	16	17
18	19	20	21	22	23	24
25	26	27	28	29	30	31

August
S	M	T	W	T	F	S
1	2	3	4	5	6	7
8	9	10	11	12	13	14
15	16	17	18	19	20	21
22	23	24	25	26	27	28
29	30	31				

September
S	M	T	W	T	F	S
			1	2	3	4
5	6	7	8	9	10	11
12	13	14	15	16	17	18
19	20	21	22	23	24	25
26	27	28	29	30		

October
S	M	T	W	T	F	S
					1	2
3	4	5	6	7	8	9
10	11	12	13	14	15	16
17	18	19	20	21	22	23
24	25	26	27	28	29	30
31						

November
S	M	T	W	T	F	S
	1	2	3	4	5	6
7	8	9	10	11	12	13
14	15	16	17	18	19	20
21	22	23	24	25	26	27
28	29	30				

December
S	M	T	W	T	F	S
			1	2	3	4
5	6	7	8	9	10	11
12	13	14	15	16	17	18
19	20	21	22	23	24	25
26	27	28	29	30	31	

FOR MORE COPIES VISIT OUR WEBSITE

www.getupandgodiary.com

OR CONTACT US ON

info@getupandgodiary.com

Postal address: **Get Up and Go Publications Ltd, Camboline, Hazelwood, Sligo, Ireland F91 NP04**.

For current prices, special offers and postal charges for your region, please refer to the website (www.getupandgodiary.com).

DIRECT ORDER FORM (please complete by ticking boxes)

PLEASE SEND ME:

The Irish Get Up and Go Diary	Year	Quantity
The Irish Get Up and Go Diary (case bound)	Year	Quantity
Get Up and Go Diary for Busy Women	Year	Quantity
Get Up and Go Diary for Busy Women (case bound)	Year	Quantity
Get Up and Go Diary	Year	Quantity
Get Up and Go Young Persons' Diary	Year	Quantity
Get Up and Go All Stars Sports Journal	Year	Quantity
Get Up and Go Daily Planner for Busy Women	Year	Quantity
Get Up and Go Gratitude Journal		Quantity
Get Up and Go Wallplanner	Year	Quantity
Get Up and Go Travel Journal		Quantity
Get Up and Go Genius Journal		Quantity
Get Up and Go Student Journal (homework journal)	Year	Quantity
Get Up and Go Heroes (all proceeds to charity)		Quantity
The Confidence to Succeed (by Donna Kennedy)		Quantity

Total number of copies

I enclose cheque/postal order for (total amount including P+P): _____

Name: _____

Address: _____

Contact phone number: _____   Email: _____

For queries, please contact us on 071 9146717/085 1764297.